Venice

Venice

Text by Anne G. Ward

Photography by F. A. H. Bloemendal

CHARLES SCRIBNER'S SONS

NEW YORK

A - 7.72 (I)

Printed in Italy
Library of Congress Catalog Card Number 73-39578
SBN 684-12920-5 (trade cloth)

Introduction

During the course of a history which can almost be counted in millennia rather than centuries, Venice has often been headline news, and in the nineteen-seventies, hundreds of years after the old city's decline from its former eminence as an undisputed world power, concern with preservation has brought it back into the public eye once more.

In the fifth century AD the low-lying islets of the lagoon, barely rising above the shallows, can have offered little intimation of the city's future greatness. The most that could be said of this inhospitable sanctuary was that for the Veneti it was infinitely preferable to facing the invaders who were overrunning the fertile lands around their cities of Padua and Aquileia. For Rome had long been deserted by ambitious men in favour of the Christian capital at Constantinople and the Roman empire in the west, disintegrating under the pressure of innumerable tensions, was finally collapsing. The barbarians were moving into Italy, sacking and looting as they came, and the cities of the Veneti lay directly in their path to Rome. Aquileia was destroyed by Attila the Hun in 453 and the Veneti, deserting their homes, took refuge on the inaccessible islands of the lagoon where there were no treasures worth plundering and no agricultural lands worth settling. For the next two hundred years they made occasional attempts to reoccupy their cities, but as the Lombards colonized the plain and tightened their grip on the surrounding countryside, the Veneti turned back to the lagoon and prepared to make a permanent home there. The problems were considerable. The land was low and swampy and there seemed to be no bedrock to provide a firm building foundation, so the people drove forests of wooden piles into the ground, added a raft of planks and perched their huts on top. Increasingly sophisticated versions of this technique have formed the supports of all subsequent buildings of Venice.

The site of the present city was not the inhabitants' first choice. Heraclea and Malamocco were the original civic centres and commerce was based on the island of Torcello. During this period the whole of the lagoon was under the sovereignty of Constantinople and the *dux*, later to be known as the Doge, was nominated directly by the Emperor. From 726 onwards he was elected by the local nobility, but imperial assent was still needed for their candidate. By the ninth century the Veneti were growing impatient of Byzantine control. They had repelled an attempt by Charlemagne's son Pepin to subjugate their territory and, becoming aware of their own power, they wanted independence. Their settlement was changing shape topographically as well as politically. The population of Torcello had been decimated by sickness, malaria was on the increase and, worst of all, the deep-water channels which brought trading vessels to the port were silting up. The decision was taken to move the mercantile settlement to the islands round Rivus Altus (deep channel), and there the market still lies, under its abbreviated modern name of Rialto.

At first no more than a group of wooden shacks precariously set on the sea-washed mudbanks round Rialto, the town was soon to receive its talisman, the focus of its pride and the object of its deepest reverence. In 828 two Venetian travellers put in at Alexandria, where they were appalled to find the relics of St Mark in the power of the infidel Turks. They abducted the body from the temple by night and managed to smuggle it out by hiding it under a load of pork, the forbidden meat which filled the Moslems with such loathing that their customs officials refused to touch the cargo. Rialto had hitherto been satisfied with the patronage of the Byzantine St Theodore whose statue still stands, one foot resting nonchalantly on a crocodile, on a column in the Piazzetta, but now piety, opportunely reinforcing nationalist sentiment as it so often does, had provided a new patron for the growing city. The first consideration was to house the relics in fitting splendour. The richer citizens had already discovered that stone houses could be erected on the dryer islands if the foundations, which sometimes cost one-third of the entire price, were made firm enough, and Byzantine craftsmen had already given impressive proofs of their mastery in the great cathedrals of Torcello and Grado. Doge Giovanni Partecipazio wanted to build a basilica for St Mark which would confirm the young republic's claim to recognition as an important independent power.

Rialto's position was not, as yet, based on any readily apparent material distinction. Business was pursued in muddy unpaved streets, the condition of which cannot have been improved by the hooves of passing horses. The people bustled energetically from the civic centre at San Marco to the trading stations of Rialto by boat, or made their way over flimsy wooden bridges, mindful of the omnipresent risk of fire, which destroyed several successive Rialto bridges and gutted the new basilica of San Marco in 976. Challenging their unprepossessing environment, they extracted salt from the water and carried on a vigorous fishing industry, the products of which were exported to Lombardy and across the Adriatic as far as Constantinople, and by 924 commerce had been greatly facilitated by the introduction of money with the minting of the *zecca* which later chroniclers call the sequin.

Venetian merchants needed more than a shrewd head for business; every trading voyage meant running the gauntlet of the pirates who infested the coasts of Croatia, and skilled seamanship and formidable armaments were essential if cargoes were to be brought safely home. In 1000 the problem came to a crisis. The Dalmatians, suffering under incessant raids which left their coasts virtually uninhabitable, appealed to the Venetians for help. A powerful fleet was mustered and led out by Doge Pietro Orseolo, who inflicted a resounding defeat on the pirates and was hailed by the grateful people as Duke of Dalmatia. Byzantine control was no more than a shadow, the pirate menace was obliterated, and the road to growth and greatness lay open. Rialto was now too slight a name for the city which ruled undisputed over the whole of the lagoon, and in the writings of Deacon Giovanni, perhaps the earliest famous man of letters produced by the town, it was given its new title: *aurea Venetia,* golden Venice.

The epithet was not undeserved. In the Middle Ages almost all the luxuries of Europe came from the east. Silks from China, spices from southeast Asia, jewels, furs, exotic woods, dyes, ivory, perfumes and gold poured into Venice in a glittering flood, and in return the city's galleys exported loads of armaments, iron and timber and carried on a flourishing trade in slaves for the harems and markets of the Moslem world. Ideally placed to act as a meeting point for overland commerce from Germany and the Danube as well as ships from the Netherlands and western Europe, Venice relied above all on its age-old connections with the Byzantine empire. As early as 715 the Venetians had occupied a privileged position in Levantine trade and by the end of the First Crusade this pre-eminence had become a virtual monopoly, for the eastern emperors had learned to fear the Crusaders as much as the Saracens, and willingly granted concessions to secure the alliance and support of the Italian commercial cities. What the Venetians could not acquire by diplomacy they took by force, and their wealth increased along with their empire.

Towards the end of the eleventh century the Basilica of San Marco was rebuilt in its present form, a fabulous blend of Byzantine opulence and Gothic splendour, to act as a private chapel for the doges. More than five hundred columns decorate the outside of the basilica, with arches, statues, mosaics, coloured stonework and the four great bronze horses on the loggia which commemorate one of Venice's most successful and reprehensible enterprises. Enrico Dandolo, a member of an old and distinguished family, was on an embassy to Constantinople when he had the misfortune to displease his hosts who, in their traditional and barbarous fashion, had his eyes put out. At the age of eighty-three the blind man was elected Doge despite his handicap, and soon afterwards the Fourth Crusade began to assemble. Venice agreed to supply transport, but when the time came to embark the Crusaders were completely unable to raise the stipulated sum. Dandolo was quick to seize his chance. He readily settled for the Crusaders' help in subduing the rebellious Venetian colony of Zara (it lay in the dominions of the Christian king of Hungary, but a city which was making a fortune selling armaments to the Saracens was not likely to be deterred from a good business deal by such considerations as that). Zara subjected, the wily and warlike Doge, stone blind and now ninety-three years of age, found no difficulty in persuading his Frankish allies to push on and attack Constantinople, which was sacked in 1204 with unbelievably bestial and destructive savagery. While the Franks ravaged the city, the Venetians methodically helped themselves to the treasures which the Byzantines had been gathering to embellish their capital ever since the great days of Greece and Rome, and among these were four magnificent horses of gilded bronze. Proud, muscular and spirited, they had been taken from Alexandria to grace the triumph of Augustus after the deaths of Antony and Cleopatra, and when Constantine adopted the Christian faith and moved his capital to Byzantium the horses went with him. Now a new conqueror took possession, and they were brought to Venice and later installed in their present location on the loggia of San Marco. Less dazzling, perhaps, but more lucrative than the bronze horses was the substantial share in the short-lived Frankish empire of Constantinople obtained by the Venetians and preserved even after the Greek Palaeologue dynasty was re-established in 1261.

While Venice's overseas empire was expanding, the pattern of government at home was also changing. To begin with, the city had been a true democracy, the Doge elected by popular consent, but this arrangement left the door open to demagogic licence on the one hand and ducal tyranny on the other, and the aristocracy took a number of steps to curb the Doge's power, so that in time he became a figurehead rather than an effective ruler. All political administration was carried out by the forty-five members of the Great Council, while executive decisions were taken by the Doge, advised and assisted by the six-man Minor Council. In 1223 the Council of Forty was formed to deal with judicial matters and in the mid-thirteenth century the Senate took control of economic affairs, and ultimately all legislation. In 1297 came the decisive step. Entry to the Great Council was limited to families which had been members during the four preceding years, and in this way a patrician class was created. The interests and well-being of the populace were so closely bound up with the patrician order that no demagogue or tyrant could hope for much support from either the ruling class or the ruled.

Inevitably there were several attempts to seize sovereign power, the first of which was so 7 feeble that it was dissipated by an old woman accidentally dropping a pot out of her window on to the head of the man who was leading the conspirators as they marched on San Marco. Abortive as this plot had proved to be, it led to the establishment of the Council of Ten, whose chief duty was to seek out and punish sedition. This sinister body, whose inquisitions and penalties were obscured in deepest mystery, went about its work with the aid of an anonymous 'post-box' in which denunciations could be secretly placed, and gradually acquired formidable powers. By the mid-fourteenth century the authority of the Ten came into direct conflict with that of the Doge, and it was the crowned head, not the citizen body, which was laid low. The octogenarian Marin Faliero was accused of plotting to overthrow the republic and seize sovereign power for himself. His plans were exposed and after a formal trial he was executed at the head of the staircase where he had received the ducal cap. The meeting-hall of the Great Council in the Palazzo Ducale has a frieze of portraits commemorating all the doges save one: where Marin Faliero's picture should be there is an inscription relating his crime and punishment in letters of gold on a black background, a macabre omission which later supplied Lord Byron with the plot of one of his less successful verse dramas.

In spite of these internal upheavals and the growing enmity of Genoa, which was challenging Venetian marine supremacy in a long-drawn-out war which sapped the city's resources, Venice in the fourteenth century was approaching the zenith of its prosperity. Directly or indirectly controlling the Dalmatian coast, a large part of Greece, Corfu and the Ionian islands, most of the Aegean and Crete in addition to its mastery of the Levantine trade, the republic boasted a fleet of nearly three thousand ships and an annual commercial profit averaging fourteen million ducats.

The Venetians possessed an undoubted aptitude for the luxury trades, which may in part have been due to their passionate love of beauty and richness. With all the wealth of the civilized world at their command they adorned their city with buildings in a style part Gothic, part Romanesque, part Byzantine and part Moorish but wholly and uniquely Venetian. Protected by the encircling water and their powerful fleet, the citizens had no need of the massive lowering fortresses which housed the great men of the rest of Europe. Their palaces are open, hospitable and gracious, triumphs of domestic elegance and comfort.

Everyone probably has an opinion as to which is the finest secular building they know, but the Palazzo Ducale of Venice must come high up on many people's lists. The early fourteenth-century south facade which gives directly on to the waterfront of St Mark's Basin is a masterpiece of harmonious rose brick and ivory stonework, daringly defying the established architectural canons by setting the solid entablature of the upper storeys above the lacy stone fretwork of the colonnade and loggia. The home of the doges was a worthy counterpart to the jewelled magnificence of the Basilica of San Marco.

The first half of the fifteenth century was the great age of palace-building among the patrician families. The Ca' d'Oro on the Grand Canal, the contract for which was signed in 1430, is a superb example of the Venetian Gothic style. The whole waterfront facade is an airy mesh of pointed arches and quatrefoil screens topped with Saracen crenellations, once rich with the gilding from which the palace took its name. Contarini, Franchetti, Garzoni, Foscari, Fasan, all the great names of Venetian history built themselves exquisite homes of marble and brick and glowing coloured stucco embellished with treasures carried home by their galleys from all over the known world. They could not know that, ironically enough, seamen as daring and enterprising as their own were bringing the end of Venice's greatness closer every day.

The ultimate collapse of the Byzantine empire, overwhelmed by the Turks in 1453, made the eastern trade routes still more difficult of access, and men began to push southwards to the Cape of Good Hope and westwards to America, seeking a new way to the fabulous riches of the Indies. The arrogance and pride of Venice in its days of power and prosperity had roused much enmity, and the other European powers began to combine against the commune on the lagoon. Its Aegean empire breaking up, Levantine trade crippled, the Turks pressing closer on the east, a hostile alliance threatening from Europe and its monopoly of the orient shattered for ever by the discoveries of Christopher Columbus, Bartolomeo Diaz and Vasco da Gama, Venice was gradually elbowed out of its dominant position in power politics. But if it could no longer force its terms on the rest of the world, a subtler victory still remained within the city's reach. Largely withdrawn from the murderous strife of Renaissance political and religious struggles, and with the vast wealth of their mercantile enterprises still at their command, the Venetians turned to the creative arts, a realm in which centuries of greatness still awaited them. It is hard to imagine a better atmosphere for fostering the pursuit of arts and letters than that of Venice, with its calm skies and lambent light and the lovely surroundings achieved wholly by man's persistence and ingenuity. The wealthy citizens had nothing better to spend their money on than patronage of beauty and the quest for pleasure, and they spent royally.

Ruskin saw the Venetian Renaissance as an unmitigated disaster, a permanent and irremediable corruption of the immaculate purity of the Gothic style—a pessimistic view by no means shared by all the city's admirers. But even if Ruskin had been right and the Renaissance had meant death to the true spirit of art in Venice, there could have been no escaping its influence. It is true that Venice had always been somewhat detached from the rest of Italy, with its own idiosyncratic manners and customs; its people speaking a soft dialect which differed markedly from the Italian of the other states; but how could the beauty-loving Venetians have remained aloof from the surge of intellectual and artistic excitement of the late fifteenth and early sixteenth centuries? In the Florence of Lorenzo the Magnificent it was said that Greek could be heard as often as Tuscan and the philosophy of Plato was worshipped as a quasi-divine revelation. In the Milan of Ludovico Sforza the urbane Leonardo da Vinci mused on the causes of things, drawing a flower, a submarine, a lock of hair or a flying machine in lines of matchless authority and significance. In the Rome of Pope Julius II an uncouth broken-nosed young man called Michelangelo, driven by the restless fury of his creative *daemon,* was bringing the Old Testament to titanic life on the ceiling of the Sistine Chapel. Venice, competitive as ever and passionately dedicated to the new and the beautiful, could not remain unaffected.

School histories often tend to speak of the Renaissance as an instantaneous explosion resulting from the influx of refugee scholars from Constantinople, but in most areas it was, in fact, a long slow maturing of the new questing spirit which could no longer tolerate the mental and physical shackles of the rigid medieval hierarchy. In Venice, however, the textbook   9 view is rather better justified than usual, for the Renaissance swept to its zenith almost within the life-span of one of its greatest exemplars, the painter Titian. His was not a short life, for he was in his late eighties or early nineties (his birth date is not known) when he died of the plague in 1576, but a mere ninety years is an amazingly brief time for so radical a movement to reach its full maturity.

The first real intimation of the rising glory of the Venetian school is to be found in the work of Giovanni, one of the sons of the wonderfully gifted Bellini family. He was among the earliest painters fully to master the new technique of working in oils, so much better suited to the moist climate of Venice than fresco or medieval tempera, but the first artists to emancipate themselves fully from the stultifying influence of the old religious canon were Bellini's two great pupils, Giorgione and Titian. A lyrical mood, alive with colour, sensuality and drama and touched by a new spirit of freedom invaded their canvases, filling the Venetian scene with light and poetry. Some clients were alarmed, more were entranced and all were amazed, and demands for Titian's work came from as far afield as France and Spain. One of his great masterpieces, the swaggering portrait of that ebullient voluptuary François I, is all the more remarkable in that it was not even painted from life but from the tiny profile on a medallion.

Tintoretto, who may have been Titian's pupil for a short time, was more widely travelled than his great predecessor, but he had only seen one other painter whose work seemed worthy of emulation. His ambition was to combine the best elements of Titian's colour with the power and impact of Michelangelo's drawing. Though few would agree that he ever equalled either master, his huge canvases have a dynamic magnetism which, unlike so much Mannerist painting, never descends to the deliberately sensational. Paolo Veronese, his contemporary, introduced a less dramatic and more measured style into his stately pictures, achieving a wonderful sense of space and light.

The Venetians, who always kept one eye firmly fixed on the practical considerations of life, were not likely to allow the more utilitarian art of architecture to be neglected, and it had two worthy exponents in Palladio, with his gracious classical pedimented facades, and Sansovino, who brought the Piazza San Marco to much of its present perfection with his designs for the Libreria Vecchia on the west of the Piazzetta and the Procuratie Vecchie along one side of the main square. The Library, one of the most admired buildings of the Renaissance, is a triumph of majestic horizontals lifted and lightened by a wealth of columns, statues and discerningly used architectural ornaments. But if Sansovino had never created anything in his entire life he would still have earned the gratitude of all civilized people, for it was his impassioned defence which saved the Palazzo Ducale from demolition after it had been badly damaged in a fire. Instead of pulling down the whole building and reconstructing from scratch in the contemporary style, as advocated by a panel of architectural advisers, the city fathers merely restored the south and west sections to their original appearance, adding a magnificent new wing on the east.

In the seventeenth century the calm classicism of the high Renaissance moved towards a more Baroque style. Palaces grew heavier and churches more ornate, culminating in Longhena's dramatic and highly personal creation of Santa Maria della Salute at the mouth of the Grand Canal. The frothy charm of German and French Rococo never really found a home in Venice, and while the rest of Europe was entering the Age of Humanism, the Serenissima

Repubblica, neither high nor dry in its lagoon backwater, was going through a period of comparative artistic stagnation—comparative because the era which successively produced Canaletto and Tiepolo can only be called stagnant if one bears in mind that Titian, Tintoretto and Veronese had all been working there little more than a century earlier.

To Europe in general Venice now represented merely another obligatory stop on the grand tour, but it was by no means the least agreeable port of call because the Venetians were now devoting their considerable superfluities of leisure and wealth to the undeviating pursuit of a good time. Apart from critical discussion of the government, which had to be avoided because it might incur the wrath of the dreaded Council of Ten, liberty and licence were extended to everyone. The people liked their creature comforts and some highly progressive measures were taken to deal with street lighting and cleaning, sanitation, public health and medical care, food and water supplies, the police force and the supervision of the quality of provisions and drugs.

The year's celebrations started with that rising crescendo of uproarious revelry which marked every carnival—indeed, festivities began even before the New Year, for permission to wear masks was announced by an outlandishly garbed government official on St Stephen's Day, December 26th. From this date until the beginning of Lent, the people of Venice, secure in the protective anonymity of the mask, could enjoy themselves exactly as they pleased. All ranks of society and walks of life mingled freely; there were masquerades and harlequinades, eating and drinking, music, singing and dancing and other notably less innocent amusements carried on in the open street with a gusto and lack of inhibition which astounded even the broadminded eighteenth century. After the riotous climax of the carnival in the last few days before Lent, the citizens took a short breathing space to recoup their forces for the celebration of Easter which, as befitted its religious nature, was conducted in a resplendent but more decorous manner. Six weeks after Easter came Ascension Day, the favourite festival of the Venetian year. For fifteen days merchants gathered in the Piazza San Marco and set up their booths under a painted, carved and gilded wooden canopy erected for the occasion. There was the usual masking and merrymaking, and then came the day itself when the Doge, attended by the nobility, embarked on the state barge or Bucintoro, a magnificent floating palace of crimson and gold rowed by sixty-eight chosen hands from the Arsenal. Accompanied by an immense flotilla of decorated boats, the Bucintoro proceeded to the Lido, where the gold ring symbolizing Venice's union with the sea was thrown into the water. The Doge then attended Mass at the church of San Niccolò del Lido and returned to the city for the state banquet at the palace, to the sound of music, church bells, salvoes of cannon fire and a general festive uproar to which the whole town liberally contributed.

Every third Sunday in July since 1576 the feast of the Redentore has been held to celebrate Venice's delivery from the plague (the festival of the Salute on November 21st was observed with similar rejoicings, but was slightly less popular, perhaps because of the colder weather). A pontoon bridge was thrown across the Grand Canal near the church of the Salute and another over the Giudecca Canal to the church of the Redentore, and all the boats in Venice, decorated with lights and greenery, anchored off the quays. All night long the people feasted, entertained by music and fireworks, and in the morning they went in procession to the Lido where they gave thanks in a religious service. The Regatta Storica was (and is) the great festival of the first Sunday in September. A procession of decorated boats bearing a pageant of Venetian history made its way along the Grand Canal, and was followed by races in the lagoon between craft representing the different parts of the commune.

If they had any spare time after preparing for (and recovering from) these feasts, the Venetians could entertain themselves at the theatre, which was immensely popular, though how it came to be so is a mystery, since the audience habitually ignored the performance, eating, drinking, chatting and flirting throughout it except when they were moved to bombard the stage with a storm of abuse, jeers, catcalls and other more tangible marks of their displeasure. Among the most riotous spectators were the gondoliers who had the privilege of free entry and free speech, both of which they exercised lustily. For those Venetians who took their music seriously, which included most of the population, there were state-subsidized choral concerts given by the orphan girls of the four great charity institutions, who sang like angels and behaved during the intervals in a conspicuously less than celestial fashion.

Naturally enough, Venice was not immune from the gambling fever which swept Europe in the seventeenth and eighteenth centuries. The government made a few ineffectual attempts to curb it and then threw their hand in and licensed the Ridotto, or gambling house, in which patricians and masked commoners impassively lost and gained vast fortunes. So many great houses were reduced to ruin by this mania that in 1744 the licence was withdrawn, and for a while the Venetians moped about the streets with long faces, at a loss to know how to pass the time. This distressing state of affairs, however, could not last long and gambling soon sprang up again in private houses, where it was pursued as avidly as ever.

On the rare occasions when these regular amusements were lacking there were dazzling festivities to mark civic, military and diplomatic successes, magnificent receptions for visiting foreign dignitaries, and the celebration of local saints' days, all of which were greeted with music, dancing and universal rejoicing. It is, indeed, quite surprising to learn that there was any time left over for the twice-yearly *villeggiatura*, when the Venetians *en masse* grew homesick for trees and grass and decamped to the mainland to spend what time they could in picnicking, playing shepherds and shepherdesses and other suitably arcadian pastimes.

The last years of the republic were passed by the Venetians in a frenzied pursuit of gaiety, wilfully deaf and blind to the gathering storm which was soon to break over France, destroying the old order for ever and taking so many ancient institutions with it. In 1797 young General Bonaparte's troops poured into Italy, invincible in the pride of their newly won democratic freedom, and although Venice offered neither obstacle nor threat, it was not spared. Napoleon wanted a bribe to placate Austria so that he could be sure his lines of communication would not be attacked, and Venice seemed the ideally tempting morsel. Manufacturing some excuse about the commune's hostility to his cause, he stormed up to the lagoon and took the city almost without resistance. On May 12th 1789 Ludovico Manin, last of 120 doges, came before the Great Council and, weeping helplessly, told them that there was no alternative but abdication and surrender. In their haste to run away, the senators voted with indecent haste for dissolution and, not with a bang but a whimper, the republic died.

Napoleon did not treat it so harshly as many conquerors might have done. He ruthlessly smashed the last of the Bucintori and sequestered many art treasures (nearly all, it is pleasant to record, faithfully restored in 1815), but there are descriptions of him watching a regatta on the Grand Canal which indicate that no calamities could keep the city in mourning for long. Under the French empire Venice was one of the seats of the Viceroy of Italy, that remarkably likeable young man, Napoleon's stepson Eugène de Beauharnais, and his wife the charming Princess Amelia Augusta of Bavaria—a pleasant couple whom hearts a good deal harder than those of the Venetians might have found it difficult to resist.

The Corsican ogre safely boxed up on St Helena, Europe breathed freely once more and borders were open again to travellers in search of culture, amusement or distraction. The last category possibly best fits the young English nobleman whose sojourn in Venice probably did more to make the city fashionable than any one individual before or since. '. . . it has always been (next to the East) the greenest island of my imagination', wrote Lord Byron to his friend Thomas Moore in November 1816. 'It has not disappointed me . . .' (*Letters and Journals*, Volume IV). Hounded out of English society (or so he liked to believe) by the resounding scandal of his broken marriage and surrounded by all the glamour of his title, his breathtaking good looks and personal charm and his undisputed poetic eminence, he came to Venice to forget the past, but the past was not in the least prepared to forget him and it is hard to say who derived the most entertainment—his lordship from Venice or Venice from his lordship. He was inevitably infected by the light-hearted mood of the city, and although he passed much of his time glooming in misanthropic isolation in the decaying splendour of the Palazzo Mocenigo, his work was beginning to branch out into an entirely new poetic form, with the sparkling vernacular narrative poem *Beppo* and the sardonic observation and mordant wit of the corrosive satire *Don Juan*.

Shelley and his wife Mary crossed Byron's path in Venice, where the two poets' evening rides and conversations on the deserted reaches of the Lido gave rise to Shelley's poetic dialogue *Julian and Maddalo*. Indeed, many of the greatest creative minds have responded in their different ways to the fascinations of the city on the lagoon and few seem to have been untouched by its magic. Charles Dickens, visiting Venice in 1844 temporarily on holiday from the restraints of his wife and rapidly increasing family, was in a receptive mood and ready to be pleased by all he saw, but even his fertile imagination had not prepared him for the experience. 'Nothing in the world that ever you have heard of Venice, is equal to the magnificent and stupendous reality', he wrote to a friend. '. . . Opium couldn't build such a place and enchantment couldn't shadow it forth . . . Venice is a bit of my brain from this time'. Elizabeth and Robert Browning, touring in 1851, changed roles for once; the relaxed atmosphere of the city and lazy days in a gondola suited the invalid Elizabeth to perfection, and it was Robert who fell ill, forcing them to leave after only a month.

It is, perhaps, just as well that some half a century or more lay between Goethe's Venetian sojourn and that of John Ruskin. Of all the sights that roused the sage of Weimar's admiration nothing moved him so profoundly as the work of Palladio. 'This is indeed something different from the crouching saints of our Gothic ornamentation . . .', he wrote. 'These, thank God, I am now rid of for ever'. Ruskin, on the contrary, saw Venice as the triumphant vindication of all his theories on the moral and spiritual values embodied in the medieval arts, and soon after the publication of *Seven Lamps of Architecture* he took his wife there to test his principles on the spot. While Mrs Ruskin wrote home to her mamma about her fabulous bargains in lace and the difficulty of getting the fire to draw properly, and dutifully echoed John's dictum that 13

Gothic is Good, her husband, passionately convinced that the new knowledge introduced during the Renaissance represented the Fall from the primeval innocence and purity of the Gothic mind, sketched, studied, measured and took casts. The result of this winter in Venice was a widening of the breach between the Ruskins and the publication in 1851 of *The Stones of Venice*, in which the city's architectural perfections are crystallized for all time in some of the noblest prose in the English language.

One of the first of the American contingent was Henry James, if that most international of writers can fairly be called American. Weaving the intricate subtleties of *The Portrait of a Lady*, he freely confessed his debt to the peculiarly generative magic of the atmosphere in his Preface. 'I had rooms on Riva Schiavoni at the top of a house near the passage leading off to San Zaccaria ; the waterside life, the wondrous lagoon spread before me, and the ceaseless human chatter of Venice came in at my windows, to which I seem to myself to have been constantly driven, in the fruitless fidget of my composition, as if to see whether, out of the blue channel, the ship of some right suggestion, of some better phrase, of the next happy twist of my subject, the next true touch for my canvas, mightn't come into sight'.

Ezra Pound, down and out in Venice in 1908 and too deeply enchanted by the city to leave, tried to supplement his tenuous finances by applying for work as a gondolier. He soon found, however, that it is nothing like so easy as it looks to control and propel thirty-six feet of streamlined sable grace in a narrow crowded canal with only the impetus of a single sweep manipulated from the standing platform near the stern. He gave up, and devoted his time to the more productive occupation of sitting on the steps of the Dogana for hours together, absorbing the influence of the scene before him as so many artists have done and will do so as long as Venice stands. Writers, poets, painters, sculptors, musicians, dancers, singers, actors, printers, jewellers ; the list is endless, and to pursue it in detail would need time and space far beyond the scope of this book.

Between Ruskin's visit and those of James and Pound a change had taken place in Venice's status which must have immeasurably revitalized the atmosphere. For the first half of the nineteenth century Venice had been driven back and forth from French pillar to Austrian post, ending as an unwilling and rebellious province of the House of Hapsburg. But the spirit of the Risorgimento was abroad, and Italians were beginning to abandon the city-state approach which had held them for centuries and think in terms of national unity. A revolt in Vienna culminating in the overthrow of the veteran statesman Metternich in 1848 provided the cue. Northern Italy rose and, under the brilliant leadership of Daniele Manin, Venice declared its independence in a bloodless revolution. Italian unity, however, was only skin deep and the support of her allies was uncertain. When the reigning Pope suddenly declared in favour of Austria and the forces of reaction, condemning the liberators out of hand, the blow to morale was incalculable. The old Austrian General Radetsky rallied his troops and re-took the north, except for Venice, which held out with all the high courage and fortitude which it had so signally failed to display during Napoleon I's invasion. Garibaldi and a few devoted volunteers rushed north to help the beleaguered city but none of them got through, and in 1849, after months of privation and cruel bombardment, Venice was forced to sue for terms. The Austrians, wisely, did not exact too harsh a price for this intransigence, but Venice's days of tame submission were over.

Austria's attempts to improve relations were ignored or actively boycotted, and when Franz Joseph took his lovely melancholic wife Elizabeth there on a goodwill mission, the imperial receptions were attended only by the members of the Austrian garrison and other resident officials. An adequate number of citizens could be rounded up to meet the illustrious visitors, but no Viennese seductions could lend a decent semblance of enthusiasm to the proceedings. In 1865 the inevitable finally came about. Bismarck formed an alliance with Victor Emmanuel against Austria and, after a desultory and undistinguished campaign, Franz Joseph was compelled to grant freedom to the Venetians, who promptly voted by plebiscite to join the rest of Italy. In October 1866 Venice at last became an Italian city.

Now a new enemy is attacking Venice—a more insidious enemy than fire or plague or foreign invader, and one against which no recourse has yet been found. The whole town is sinking, slowly but inexorably, into the waterlogged sands of the lagoon. The wash and vibration of modern motor-driven craft are accelerating the process; injections of concrete into the ancient foundations can only add to the weight and increase the rate of subsidence, and all the expertise of some of the world's greatest hydraulic engineers has not yet devised a way to halt the city's dissolution. However, no one who lives in this century, which has seen man's first clumsy attempts at flight develop into the conquest of space, would dare to say that any question cannot be solved, and so long as scientists of imagination and tenacity of purpose are working on the problem, Venice need not despair of a solution.

The matter is one of great urgency, for the city has so much to offer. It is so old, so beautiful and so different that it is not so much a town as a unique experience. No words can tell what Venice is like, because there is nothing like it in the whole of the world. Many other towns have been named 'the Venice of the north', or south, or west, or anywhere else for that matter, but one look at the original is enough to dispel any such comparisons for ever. Its contribution to cultivated life has been immeasurable. Every one of the major arts has owed a debt to it in the person of some distinguished exponent, and who can say how many of the minor urbanities of life are to be traced back there? Not many people realize, for instance, that one of the first recorded Europeans to use a fork at table instead of a knife and bare hands was the wife of Doge Pietro Orseolo II as early as the eleventh century. It is curious to reflect that Louis XIV, for all the pompous magnificence of his state banquets, was still eating with his fingers at a time when the Venetians had been using forks for hundreds of years. A trivial detail, but it takes very little imagination to show what a difference this small convenience must have made to the general seemliness of domestic life.

While the scientists fight to save it, Venice's best friend is the photographer, whose art alone can do something to capture its incomparable bewitchments for all time. A single good picture, created with the eye of love and understanding, can convey more about the city than whole libraries full of written words, and can help to perpetuate the loveliness which seems to be condemned to extinction.

It will not be this year, nor next, nor for many years to come. But sooner or later Venice must be saved from the water whence it rose in triumph so many centuries ago.

Anne G. Ward 15

The fortunate visitor is the one who arrives by water from the lagoon and sees the full splendour of the Bacino di San Marco as his introduction to Venice. To the right are the white stone buildings of the prison and next to this comes the glory of the city, the exquisite Gothic Palazzo Ducale. Across the spacious expanse of the Piazetta, with its two lofty columns, rears the huge tower of the Campanile behind Sansovino's Library. Abutting on the Library and flanked by the public gardens is the Zecca, a noble and severe structure also by Sansovino built in 1536 to house the Mint of Venice.

16

The Piazza San Marco is the heart of Venice and is never seen without a crowd of eager sightseers and local strollers braving the swarms of pigeons to enjoy the pleasures of its spacious elegance. The southwest corner of the Palazzo Ducale, carved with an attractive Adam and Eve, projects in the foreground in front of the south face of St Mark's Basilica. In the background are the Torre dell' Orologio and the Procuratie Vecchie, which once housed the custodians of the fabric of St Mark's. On festive occasions the flagstaffs fly immense red and gold banners reaching nearly the full height of the poles.

The beautiful facade of St Mark's Basilica is dominated by two tiers of arches, each of which is filled by a mosaic on a golden ground. Only the left-hand arch still has the original Byzantine work; the central mosaic, showing the Last Judgment, was not installed till 1836 and in some ways forms a curious contrast with the hieratic stateliness of the earlier piece. The other panels all depict scenes which were particularly appealing to Venetian taste as they tell the story of the translation of the body of St Mark from Alexandria to Venice.

On a corner of the Basilica of San Marco adjoining the Doges' Palace stand two pairs of small embracing figures carved in porphyry, the imperial stone of the later Roman Empire. They are the Tetrarchs—the joint rulers (*Augusti*) of the empire and their two junior co-regents (*Caesares*), whose unity, usually more hoped for than real, was symbolized by their embrace. Revolt from the classical canon of ideal beauty is expressed by the uncompromising realism with which the sculptor has invested the coarse, sullen forms of Diocletian and Maximian (right) and their younger associates Galerius and Constantius Chlorus.

On the loggia above the central door of St Mark's Basilica stand the four bronze horses looted from Constantinople by the Venetians during the Fourth Crusade. Their former gilding is almost worn away, their flanks are streaked with the green marks of weathering and various barbarians have perpetuated their own disgrace by scratching their names on the metal, but the splendour of their proud grace is undimmed although it is two thousand years since they left the studio of the Greek sculptor who made them in Alexandria. Commandeered by Napoleon, whose rapacity for art treasures was only equalled by that of the Venetians themselves, they were replaced in 1815, and though they underwent a similar fate in 1914-18 and 1939-45 they have always returned to their place on the loggia.

Opposite the colonnade of Sansovino's Library on the west of the Piazzetta stand two tall columns of oriental granite. The one nearest the palace bears a metal sculpture of a lion perhaps dating from the Sassanid era which was remodelled to represent the Lion of St Mark. Beyond the columns extends the beautiful facade of the Palazzo Ducale. Badly damaged by fire in the sixteenth century, a council of architects called in to debate the renovation of the palace loudly called for demolition and total rebuilding with true Renaissance passion for novelty, and only the opposition of Sansovino, as determined as it was discriminating, saved this loveliest of civic structures.

In the Renaissance great extensions were added to the Gothic Doges' Palace. Beyond a well-head in the northeast corner of the courtyard of the palace is the Giants' Staircase (Scala dei Giganti), a splendid ascent beautifully decorated by Rizzo (1484-1501). Two huge statues of Mars and Neptune by Sansovino guard the top of the steps where the Doge-elect was crowned with the *corno ducale*. The earlier stairway of the palace had been the site of a grimmer ceremony in which Marin Faliero, a renegade Doge who had tried to invest his elective office with all the powers of a tyrant, was beheaded in 1355 by the order of the council.

The narrow canal running between the Palazzo Ducale and the prisons is spanned by the Ponte della Paglia, which was built in 1360 and widened in 1847—a very necessary improvement as it supplies the only view of the Bridge of Sighs and is always crowded with avid sightseers and photographers. At the base of the Ponte della Paglia is a small shrine known as the Tabernacolo della Fraglia del Traghetto, which houses the graceful little sixteenth-century relief figure of the 'Madonna of the Gondoliers'.

30

'I stood in Venice, on the Bridge of Sighs', wrote Lord Byron in *Childe Harold's Pilgrimage*—a difficult feat since the bridge is roofed in and though one can stand *in* the bridge, it would need a considerable feat of gymnastics to stand on it. However, if his lordship's topographical observation was faulty, his poetic appreciation was unerring and his wonderfully apt name for the bridge has been universally adopted. Built by Antonio Contino about 1600, it leads from the interrogation room in the Palazzo Ducale (on the left) to the prisons, and those who passed through it had, indeed, plenty to sigh about, although the prisons of Venice were considered a model of humani-tarian detention by contemporaries.

32

From the Campanile in St Mark's Square a view over the rooftops of the city includes the top of the Torre dell' Orologio (clock tower) built by Mauro Coducci in 1496-9. The enormous clock face, with its complex astrological signs (it tells the time of day only incidentally), is surmounted by a figure of the Madonna, and above her on a blue and gold background is the lion of St Mark. Two bronze figures known as the *mori* (Moors), installed in 1497, strike the hours on the great bell that crowns the tower.

34

Looking over the rooftop of the Palazzo Ducale from the Campanile in St Mark's Square, the waterfront of the Riva degli Schiavoni presents a picture of lively activity. In the foreground is the landing stage of the vaporetto, the water-borne bus of Venice, just beyond which a row of tugs are moored, awaiting a summons to fetch big shipping into the lagoon from the Adriatic. Beyond the bridge over the Rio dell' Arsenale, a cruise liner, one of the many luxury ships making a short stop at this most attractive of ports, awaits its passengers.

The wide walk along the waterfront from the Palazzo Ducale to the Arsenal is named the Riva degli Schiavoni, from the fact that it was once the centre for the merchants from Dalmatia (*Schiavia*—Slavia). It still preserves a connection with that coast, as the hydrofoils running excursions from Split and other Yugoslav ports are often to be seen moored along the quay. The most conspicuous monument on the Riva is an exuberant bronze equestrian statue of Victor Emmanuel II set up in 1887 to commemorate the unification of Italy and the liberation of Venice from Austrian domination.

The Bacino di San Marco and the Riva degli Schiavoni, seen from the campanile of San Giorgio Maggiore, are a typically Venetian blend of crowded activity and serene architectural beauty. On the right is the waterfront church of the Pietà, to the left of which the tower of San Giorgio dei Greci leans alarmingly over a narrow canal. The background on the left is dominated by the vast brick bulk of the church of San Zanipólo (Giovanni e Paolo). On the waterfront, to the left, stands an elaborate and grandiose but somewhat unprepossessing monument to Victor Emmanuel II.

The church and monastery of San Giorgio Maggiore stand on a small island directly across the Bacino di San Marco from the Palazzo Ducale. Rebuilt in 1566-80 by Palladio with a few finishing touches added in 1610 by Scamozzi, the church is a handsome example of the classic Renaissance style. To the left of the church is the sailing ship belonging to the naval cadets' establishment and behind it are the quiet gardens which contain a charming open-air theatre built by Count Cini in memory of his son, who was killed in an air crash.

42

Towards the eastern end of the lagoon waterfront is the Arsenal of Venice, an eighty-acre site surrounded by crenellated brick walls and towers. The splendid Renaissance gateway by Gambello is surmounted by a statue of Saint Justina and defended on every side by lions, emblem of the city's patron St Mark. Two were sent to Venice from Athens by Francesco Morosini, conqueror of the Morea, in 1692 and two more were added after the relief of Corfu. Runic characters inscribed on the early Greek lion from Delos attest the presence of the Vikings in the Mediterranean.

One of the finest hotels in Venice is the Danieli, which stands on the waterfront near the Palazzo Ducale. Apart from the distinction lent by the innumerable stars which follow its name in the tour books, it is a fifteenth-century building of some dignity, with a fine loggia topped with a row of handsome quatrefoils. Doyen of the city's *alberghi,* it is known for having extended its hospitality to such renowned visitors as George Sand and Alfred de Musset (who quarrelled disastrously during their ill - fated Venetian 'honeymoon'), Charles Dickens and John Ruskin.

46

At the mouth of the Grand Canal is a narrow point of land with the church of San Gregorio, the great Baroque church of Santa Maria della Salute and the long, low buildings of the Dogana. Beyond the point is the Guidecca Canal, the deep-water channel which takes big ships round to the industrial docks at the end of Venice nearest the mainland, and then comes the narrow island of Guidecca, now largely an industrial suburb of Venice, which owes its name to the belief that the Jewish population of the city was once required to live there.

From the top of the wooden Accademia bridge over the Grand Canal the church of Santa Maria della Salute and the handsome Dogana (customs house) can be seen on the right. Built by Longhena (1631-81), this imposing Baroque church was Venice's thanks-offering after a visitation of the plague, which was a fairly frequent infliction in the days before a good water supply was piped into the city from the Dolomites. The long, low structure of the Dogana, roughly contemporary with the Salute and built by Benoni, ends in a tower topped with a gilded ball supporting a weather-vane in the form of a figure of Fortuna.

The argument for and against the reconstruction of ancient buildings is never likely to be decisively solved, but in Venice there is less to be said against it than almost anywhere else. A fine example of what a generous and discerning restorer can do is to be seen in the Palazzo Cavalli Franchetti, which stands in well tended and unusually extensive gardens at the foot of the Accademia bridge. This magnificent fifteenth-century palace with its double loggia in the same style as that of the Palazzo Ducale was repaired in 1890 by Camillo Boito, and is now one of the most prosperous looking and best preserved houses in Venice.

52

One of the earliest and probably the most beautiful of the private palaces in Venice is the Ca' d'Oro, so named from the gilding which once adorned the stonework on the facade. It was built by the Buon family in 1421-36 for the great merchant princes of the house of Contarini, but its glory declined for centuries until in the nineteen-hundreds it fell into the hands of the famous ballet dancer Taglioni. As a great creative artist herself, she should have known better, but she set about 'improving' the palace till its interior was little more than a wreck and it was only saved by the generosity of Baron Franchetti, who bought it, restored it and presented it to the city.

54

Practically next door to the exquisite Ca'
d'Oro is the rather confused architecture of
the Palazzo Sagredo, now the Istituto Rava,
fenced in by the mooring poles of a *traghetto*. Built in the fourteenth century, the
palace incorporates some Venetian Byzantine elements, with a row of fine pointed
arches over the first-floor balcony. Like so
many Venetian buildings, it displays flourishing window-boxes which give a touch of
freshness and colour to the slightly dilapi-
dated exterior and go far to make up for
the lack of garden space. Beyond the palace
the Grand Canal curves away towards the
Rialto bridge.

Dominating a bend in the Grand Canal is the Palazzo Balbi, a Renaissance palace designed in 1582-90 by Vittorio. The advancing tide of Baroque influence is apparent in the slightly heavy architectural ornament surrounding the windows from which Napoleon once watched a regatta, and in the two obelisks decorating the rooftop. On its right are palaces of the Grimani and Dandolo families, with a strictly twentieth - century touch in the vaporetto landing-stage of San Tomà.

On the west side of the Grand Canal between the Accademia and the Rialto is the Palazzo Papadopoli, formerly Coccina-Tiepolo (on the right), an imposing building in the classic Renaissance style attributed to Grigi, and one of the few to boast possession of a small waterside garden. Next to it, the two Donà palazzi are served by the Traghetto della Madonnetta, and to the left is the Palazzo Grimani, one of the finest and handsomest of the Venetian palaces in the Lombard style.

Every visitor and resident in Venice at some time or other passed over, under or around the famous Rialto bridge, the fine stone arch spanning the Grand Canal. It is crowded with little shops, mostly selling rather lamentable souvenirs, which distract attention from the stonework.

62

Built in 1588-92 by the appropriately named Antonio da Ponte, the Rialto was the first stone bridge on this site, which had previously been served by a pontoon bridge (until 1264) and a wooden structure. Reliefs of saints and angels by Aspetti decorate the spaces at each end of the span.

64

Immediately beside the bustle and uproar of the Rialto market is the church of San Giacomo di Rialto, reputedly the oldest in Venice. Tradition ascribes its foundation to the fifth or sixth century, but the main structure belongs to the eleventh to twelfth centuries with extensive reconstructions carried out in 1601. The Gothic portico has a wooden architrave supported by five columns (the only example of its kind in the city), and the facade is completely dominated by a large and resplendent clock above which is a delightful Gothic Madonna

and Child dating to the fifteenth century.

Round the next corner of the Grand Canal
north of the Rialto bridge are the markets of
Venice where fruit and vegetables from the
mainland, seafood from the lagoon and
tourist souvenirs from practically everywhere
are sold in a pleasantly noisy, jostling con-
fusion. The site of the oldest of the market
buildings, immediately across the canal from
the Palazzo Foscari, does not present nearly
so undignified an outlook to that patrician
structure as might be expected. The 'old'
market is a handsome colonnade with a
loggia above it built by Rufolo in 1907 after

a design by Laurenti.

A small canal running inland at right angles on the west side of the Grand Canal supplies access to the fish markets of Venice, which are housed in an elegant Gothic-style colonnade built early in the twentieth century after a design by the Ferrarese painter Laurenti. In the mornings when business is in full swing the market is a visual delight, with piles of exotic silver, pink, green and blue-black marine life artfully arranged on sprays of fresh greenery, but the area behind the stalls, though almost equally picturesque, is distinctly less pleasing to the nose than to the eye.

Towards the north end of the Grand Canal stands the Fondaco dei Turchi, once one of the finest Romanesque palaces in Venice. Built in the thirteenth century for the Pésaro family, from 1621 onwards it was the Venetian trading-post of the Turks, who carried on a flourishing business there regardless of the state of hostilities existing between Ottoman and Christian. By the mid-nineteenth century the Fondaco had fallen into a state of sad decay, and repairs and restorations were unfortunately carried out with a rather crude and heavy hand. It now houses the Museum of Natural History.

72

The Ponte di Cannaregio (or Guglie—so many places in Venice have an alternative name, always conscientiously given on the street signs) which gives on to the Rio Terà San Leonardo is a handsome bridge dating to 1580 and reconstructed in 1776, with stone mask decorations and an obelisk at each corner. The wide Cannaregio canal which it spans cuts through from the Grand Canal to the north shore of Venice, and before the building of the causeway was the main access route to Mestre and the mainland.

74

The Campo della Maddalena near the north end of the Grand Canal is a typical Venetian square. A group of pleasant little houses was once served by the early fifteenth-century well-head (now fortunately superseded by an abundant supply of healthy piped water) resembling a classical column capital. On the left is the facade of the Chiesa della Maddalena, a curious church of almost circular shape designed by Temanza in the mid-eighteenth century. The street which gives access to the square is a *rio terà*, a name which indicates a filled-in canal.

There are only three bridges over the Grand Canal: the Accademia, the Rialto and, right down at the mainland end of the city, the Ponte degli Scalzi. Beside the bridge is the Scalzi church, a handsome Baroque structure built by Longhena in 1670-80. The efficient modern railway station next to the church is officially called Venezia-Santa Lucia because it stands on the site of the church which once housed the relics of St Lucy, a pious Sicilian of Diocletian's time who was done to death for adhering to her vow not to marry, which she evidently regarded as the worse martyrdom of the two.

In the afternoons large numbers of Venetians can be seen converging on the Campo San Zanipolo. Crossing the Rio dei Mendicanti by a bridge bearing a plaque enjoining passing boatmen to silence, they turn left to pass through the handsome Scuola Grande di San Marco to the civic hospital. One of the finest Renaissance buildings in Venice, it was erected in 1488-90 by Pietro Lombardo and Giovanni Buora, with additions to the upper part made in 1500 by Coducci. A statue of Charity surmounts the ornate doorway and, not surprisingly, the lion of St Mark is very much in evidence on the facade.

Venice has its own words for many things which are not in general use in Italian. A boatyard there is known as a *squero,* and devotes as much of its time to the maintenance of gondolas as to more mundane craft. The *squero* on the Rio di San Trovaso is one of the most picturesque in Venice, with its ancient balconied boathouse next to the sixteenth - century church of San Trovaso. It also boasts the neighbourhood of one of the rarest amenities in the city— a small open space of grass and trees.

One of the finest statues in Venice is the bronze monument to the great Renaissance *condottiere* Bartolomeo Colleoni (c. 1400-75) in Campo San Zanipólo. The figure was begun by Verrocchio and finished after his death by Leopardi. It stands outside the church of SS. Giovanni e Paolo which, with the Frari, is one of the finest Venetian brick churches in the Gothic order. It is known as the Pantheon of the Doges because it contains the tombs of so many of the city's greatest rulers. The Dominicans initiated the construction of this massive edifice in 1246 and it was not ready for dedication until 1430.

Along with glassworking, the making of lace has been one of the most famous and lucrative Venetian crafts for many years. During the eighteenth century the industry decayed, but it was given a timely new lease of life by the foundation in 1872 of the Scuola dei Merletti, or lacemakers' school, under the patronage of the Dogaressas, in the quiet little fishing village of Burano. Faced by competition from modern mass-produced lace, the Venetian handmade article still keeps its pre-eminence and the women of Burano continue to produce it in their own homes.

Beyond the landing where tourists embark every evening in gondolas for the musical tour of the city known as the night serenade stands the Baroque church of San Moisè with its heavy ornate facade built by Alessandro Tremignon in 1668. The church's greatest claim to international fame is the grave of the financier John Law, whose enticing but ill-founded economic theories so beguiled the young Louis XV of France that he almost brought the country to bankruptcy.

A small bridge over a little canal on 'the other side of the Grand Canal' (as one tends to call the west side) leads to the Scuola di San Rocco with its wonderful collection of paintings and to the nearby Frari church, a marvellous Gothic brick church where Titian lies buried and where his Assumption of the Madonna crowns the high altar. The whole neighbourhood is full of pleasant little corners, quiet canals and ancient Gothic courtyards and, being slightly removed from the main tourist haunts, is less crowded and commercialized than some of the better known areas.

Almost every inch of ground in Venice is man-made, and if very little can be spared for gardens, none at all is available for growing foodstuffs. These, however, are ferried in from the mainland by the innumerable boats of every shape and size which take the place of all wheeled vehicles from buses and cycles to petrol tankers and pantechnicons. This has one notable advantage; the city is completely cut off from the use of anything which cannot be moved by water and carried by manpower, so that everything is kept down to a refreshingly human scale of size and speed.

92

The island of Murano is still the centre of the glassworking industry upon which so much of the commercial success of Venice has always rested. At present the island houses only the factories and the homes of the craftsmen, but in former times it enjoyed considerable prestige. Catherine Cornaro, Queen of Cyprus, had a villa there, and a distinguished school of painters under the leadership of Antonio Vivarini flourished in the mid-fifteenth century. One of the few relics of former glory is the magnificent seventh - century Byzantine basilica of SS. Maria e Donato with its fine arcaded apse and free-standing campanile.

In 1870, with the coming of the railways to Venice via the mile-long causeway which connects the city with the mainland, it was decided that no adequate streets existed between the station and the Rialto area. Accordingly, several canals were filled in to provide a direct walk. Among these was the present Rio Terà San Leonardo, now a broad and busy street lined with shops and sidewalk cafés, which forms part of the link between the Lista di Spagna near the station and the Strada Nova near the Rialto.

96

Not far north of the Rialto is the church of San Giovanni Crisostomo, behind which lies the modern restaurant incorporating the remains of Marco Polo's home. The Ponte dell'Olio which spans the Rio dei Tedeschi gives a view of one of the innumerable picturesque corners of Venice, where several narrow canals, flanked by tall houses with Gothic-arched windows and the inevitable green or brown shutters, meander through the byways of the city.

If the Grand Canal is the backbone of Venice, the bridges are surely its ribs. Many people think of the city as an island dissected by innumerable canals but it is, in fact, more than a hundred islands, sandbanks and shoals joined by at least three hundred bridges over its 150 waterways. Bridge-building is far from easy on the soft, shifting ground which offers no firm resistance to the lateral thrust of the arch, and all the larger ones are based on an elaborate sub-structure of piles set at different angles above the foundation raft.

The topography of Venice allows only two forms of locomotion—walking and boating. It is ideally suited to both of these means, the former because of the enforced absence of wheeled transport in the narrow streets and over the stepped bridges, which makes it a real pleasure to stroll and stare by the hour together undisturbed by the motor menace which is rapidly overrunning the rest of Italy. As to the canals, many dire comments on the smells have been made by people who forget that there is a tide in the Venice lagoon even if it is scarcely noticeable, so that the water is far from being completely stagnant.

Not all the *squeri* of Venice are as picturesque as that of San Trovaso. The Rio dei Mendicanti, which runs inland from the Fondamente Nuove, is the site of several hardworking little boatyards servicing the local shallow-draught barges as well as fishing boats and gondolas. Every family of note once had its own private gondola, and great competition existed between them in the decoration of these graceful and elegant craft. At length so much money was being squandered that in 1562 the senate was obliged to pass a decree requiring that they should all be painted black, and so they still remain.

Since the earliest foundation of the city the basis of its domestic economy has always been the fishing industry. Every citizen who owns anything that floats spends a good deal of his time dredging marine life out of the lagoon, all of which seems to be edible and delicious. One of the most characteristic local dishes of the region consists of tiny fish, shrimp, mussels, pieces of squid, baby octopus and other less identifiable but equally delectable oddments crisply fried and served with lemon. Pollution experts are loudly preaching their counsels of despair and it is true that all garbage from washing-up water to old prams seems to be heedlessly dumped into the lagoon, but—as yet—the sea continues to supply a seemingly inexhaustible fund of delicacies.

From the fifth century to the thirteenth, the island of Torcello in the eastern part of the lagoon was the centre of a trading community and at the height of its power it boasted 20,000 inhabitants. Now there is only a small village among the trees and fields but a relic of Torcello's great days still survives in the form of the vast early Byzantine cathedral founded in 639 and reconstructed in 864 and 1008. Behind the cathedral, completely detached from it, stands the campanile and next to it is the eleventh - century octagonal church of Santa Fosca which is now the village church of the community.

108

The waterfront of the island of San Giorgio Maggiore provides a vantage point for one of the finest views in Venice. On the right the rosy brickwork of the Doges' Palace rises above the exquisite Gothic colonnades of the loggia and on the other side of the Piazzetta is Sansovino's great Library, considered by Palladio to be one of the most beautiful buildings of the age. The 325 foot Campanile is a copy of the original Renaissance tower which collapsed in 1902. It seems typical of the urbane and civilized mood of the city that when the Campanile fell it did not cause a single injury.